Geronimo Stilton
ACADEMY

Grammar Pawbook 2

Text by Geronimo Stilton
Based on the original idea by Elisabetta Dami
Illustrations by Piemme Archives

www.geronimostilton.com

© Atlantyca S.p.A. – via Leopardi 8, 20123 Milano, Italia – foreignrights@atlantyca.it

© 2016 for this Work in English language, Scholastic Education International (Singapore) Private Limited. A division of Scholastic Inc.
SCHOLASTIC and associated logos are trademarks and/or registered trademarks of Scholastic Inc.

Visit our website: www.scholastic.com.sg

First edition 2016

ISBN 978-981-4629-95-9

Stilton is the name of a famous English cheese. It is a registered trademark of the Stilton Cheese Makers' Association. For more information go to www.stiltoncheese.com

Welcome to the
Geronimo Stilton
ACADEMY

Well-loved for its humor, fascinating visuals, and fun characters, the best-selling *Geronimo Stilton* series is enjoyed by children in many countries.

Research shows that learners learn better when they are engaged and motivated. The **Geronimo Stilton Academy: Grammar Pawbook** series builds on children's interest in Geronimo Stilton. It makes learning more accessible, and increases learners' motivation to read and strengthen their grammar skills.

The Geronimo Stilton Academy: Grammar Pawbook series comprises three levels:

Pawbook 1 (Junior level)	Pawbook 2 (Senior level)	Pawbook 3 (Master level)
• Explanation of grammar items • Word and sentence level activities • Includes - common and proper nouns - simple sentences - simple present tense - modal verbs	• Explanation of grammar items • Sentence and short text level activities • Includes - subject-verb agreement - the to-infinitive - adjective placement - quantifiers	• Explanation of grammar items • Sentence and text level activities • Includes - indefinite pronouns - gerunds - active and passive voice - complex sentences

Please refer to the contents page for a full list of topics.

Geronimo Stilton titles featured in this Pawbook:

© 2016 Scholastic Education International (S) Pte Ltd   ISBN 978-981-4629-95-9

Motivating learners
Authentic excerpts from *Geronimo Stilton* titles interest and encourage learners to read the rest of the story.

Reinforcing grammar skills
The 3-step format in each unit explains grammar items used in context, and provides opportunities for learners to reinforce their grammar skills.

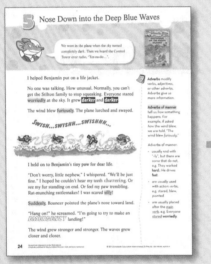
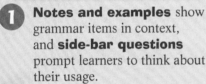

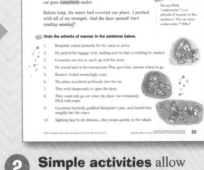

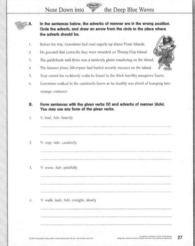

1 **Notes and examples** show grammar items in context, and **side-bar questions** prompt learners to think about their usage.

2 **Simple activities** allow learners' to assess their basic understanding of grammar items.

3 **Sentence and text level activities** help reinforce learners' understanding and usage of grammar items.

Consolidating learning
Each double-page spread consists of an activity related to the preceding units to help consolidate what students have learned.

© 2016 Scholastic Education International (S) Pte Ltd   ISBN 978-981-4629-95-9

Contents

© 2016 Scholastic Education International (S) Pte Ltd ISBN 978-981-4629-95-9

1 We Are in Big Trouble!

A mysterious one-eyed rat was trying to ruin *The Rodent's Gazette* and Stilton Publishing! What were we going to do?

I couldn't take the stress anymore. Things were moving fast. **TOO FAST**. Faster than a hamster on a treadmill. Faster than being chased by a cat. Faster than New Mouse City's annual rat race!

I FAINTED. Mousella took a piece of blue cheese and **waved** it under my nose. The strong smell woke me up. I could hear my staff members muttering.

"Who is this mysterious rat?"

"Why does he want to ruin *The Rodent's Gazette*?"

I came to my senses. What kind of a mouse was I? My staff needed me. I had to be strong.

"**QUIET!**" I shouted. Everyone stared at me.

"It's true. We are in big trouble," I said. "But that just means we have to be strong. We have to stay calm. There is a solution for every problem. We will get through this!"

Everyone cheered. Then **DUSTY DUSTWELL**, the cleaning lady, spoke up. "Great speech, Mr. Stilton. So what do we do now?"

I smoothed my fur. I wiggled my ears. I cleared my throat. I opened my mouth to speak … and burst into tears!

Nouns can be singular or plural. **Singular nouns** mean there is only one. Plural nouns mean there are many.

Most **plural nouns** are formed by adding "s" to the end of the word. The exceptions:

- For nouns that end in "ch", "x", "s", or s sounds, add "-es".

- For nouns that end in "y", change the "y" to "ies". If there is a vowel before the "y", just add an "s". So, the plural of "boy" is "boys", but the plural of "candy" is "candies".

- Some have different plural forms, e.g. the plural of "mouse" is "mice".

Excerpt from *Watch Your Whiskers, Stilton!*
(Originally published in Italy by Edizioni Piemme *Attenti ai baffi … arriva Topigoni*)

© 2016 Scholastic Education International (S) Pte Ltd   ISBN 978-981-4629-95-9

We Are in 🧀 Big Trouble!

"I don't knooooooooooooooooooooooooooo"
I wailed.

I fell to the floor, crying. Through my sobs,
I could hear the other mice talking about me.

"Poor Mr. Stilton!"

"After all he has *DONE* for the company."

"What will Cheap Mouse Willy have to say about this?"

"I am sure he will do something TERRIBLE to
Geronimo!"

"This is worse than a hunk of Swiss cheese with
no holes!"

"Worse than being caught in a rattrap!"

"Worse than a cheeseburger with no cheese!"

"Slimy Swiss rolls, I'm glad I'm not in Mr. Stilton's fur
right now!"

Chew on it!

What are the plural forms for the following words: trouble, speech, company?

🧀 **Match each singular noun to its plural form.**

1.	baby	•	•	monkeys
2.	throat	•	•	cheeses
3.	watch	•	•	cities
4.	monkey	•	•	children
5.	tooth	•	•	buses
6.	cheese	•	•	races
7.	child	•	•	solutions
8.	day	•	•	babies
9.	bus	•	•	watches
10.	solution	•	•	teeth
11.	race	•	•	days
12.	city	•	•	throats

© 2016 Scholastic Education International (S) Pte Ltd ISBN 978-981-4629-95-9

Excerpt from Watch Your Whiskers, Stilton!
(Originally published in Italy by Edizioni Piemme Attenti ai baffi ... arriva Topigoni)

A. **When a singular noun ends with an "f" or "fe", the plural form is different. You change the "f" to a "v" and follow that with "es". For example, "loaf" becomes "loaves" and "life" becomes "lives". Fill in each blank with the plural form of a word in the box.**

newspaper	squeak	knife	joke
book	shelf	daisy	bench

1. Geronimo was puzzled. The _____ he published were not in the bookstores!

2. He felt like someone decided to stab him, and had stuck many _____ into his back.

3. Even the newsstand did not carry his _____.

4. Thea strolled into the park and saw a few _____. She sat on one.

5. Thea saw some lovely flowers and picked a bunch of

   _____ for herself.

6. He looked at the clock hanging next to the _____ and realized that he was late for a meeting.

7. As he stood in the empty hallway, he heard loud _____.

8. Benjamin told Geronimo many _____, and made him laugh.

B. **Some nouns keep the same form, whether they are singular or plural, e.g. "sheep". Circle the correct singular or plural noun in the sentences below.**

1. Benjamin is watching a documentary about a family of (deer / deers).

2. Geronimo bought some (furniture / furnitures) for his office.

3. The young mouse bought three new pairs of (pant / pants).

4. They discovered one new (specie / species) of rodent.

5. To lure the cat out, they decided to use a few (salmon / salmons) as bait.

Excerpt from *Watch Your Whiskers, Stilton!*
(Originally published in Italy by Edizioni Piemme *Attenti ai baffi ... arriva Topigoni*)

We Are in Big Trouble!

For singular nouns that end with "o", you add either an "s" or "es" to get the plural form. For example, "piano" becomes "pianos", and "hero" becomes "heroes". Fill in each blank with either the singular or plural noun of a word from the box. Each word should only be used once.

scissors	voice	bread	desk
carpet	letter	leaf	tree

Leona Misermouse is the owner of the building where *The Rodent's Gazette's* offices are located. She sent Geronimo a number of _____ 1 asking him to leave the building. Geronimo was so upset he wailed at the top of his _____ 2 for his secretary, Mousella. She told him to look out the window at the few cherry _____ 3 across the road to calm down. The trees had shed so many _____ 4 from their branches that it made a _____ 5 of green on the pavement. Looking at the trees did help Geronimo feel better.

Meanwhile, Mousella went to the market to buy some _____ 6 to make a cheese sandwich. When she got back to the office, she found, on her _____ 7, a box with three pairs of _____ 8 in it. She was surprised, but she appreciated the useful tools.

© 2016 Scholastic Education International (S) Pte Ltd ISBN 978-981-4629-95-9

Excerpt from *Watch Your Whiskers, Stilton!*
(Originally published in Italy by Edizioni Piemme *Attenti ai baffi … arriva Topigoni*)

We were in danger of losing *The Rodent's Gazette*. We needed help. Who better to turn to than our old business manager, Shif T. Paws …

The door flew open. It slammed into my snout, crushing my whiskers. I stuck to the door like cheese on pizza. Then I slid to the floor and fainted.

Mousella revived me with more blue cheese. I opened my eyes and saw *the mouse* who had flung the door open.

He was a tall rodent wearing a gray suit and striped tie. The top of his head was as round and FURLESS as a ball of mozzarella. Wire-rimmed glasses perched on the tip of his snout. Cell phones hung all over him like ornaments on a Christmas tree. He had a YELLOW cell phone behind his right ear, a RED cell phone in the pocket of his jacket, a BLUE one in his shirt pocket, a GREEN one in his back pants pocket, and a PINK cell phone hung around his neck.

"Shif!" I CRIED, bouncing up to my paws. "It's great to see you again." …

Shif T. had left us a year ago to pursue a business opportunity in Ratzikistan, selling ice to Eskimice. Only a salesmouse like Shif T. could pull something like that off. …

Shif T.'s EYES shone behind his glasses. "Are you all with me? Come on, it's selling time!" he yelled.

Nouns can be countable or uncountable. **Countable nouns** are those that we can count using numbers. We use:

- "one", "a", or "an" with the singular form, e.g. one door
- a number with the plural form, e.g. two paws.

Uncountable nouns are those we cannot count with numbers. They include:

- abstract nouns, e.g. spirit, honesty
- physical objects that are too small (e.g. sand) or have no clearly-defined shape (e.g. water)
- energy forces, e.g. sunshine.

We usually use determiners like "some" and "much" or phrases like "a bit of" for uncountable nouns.

 Excerpt from *Watch Your Whiskers, Stilton!*
(Originally published in Italy by Edizioni Piemme *Attenti ai baffi … arriva Topigoni*)

© 2016 Scholastic Education International (S) Pte Ltd ISBN 978-981-4629-95-9

The staff was silent for a moment. They all LOOKED at one another.

Then they cried out, "HURRAH for Shif T. Paws!"

"That's the spirit!" Shif T. shouted. "We will save *The Rodent's Gazette*!"

Everyone cheered. Then Shif T. suddenly looked upset.

"Crusty keypads!" Shif T. shrieked. "I've lost my favorite cell phone!"

The salesmouse RAN out of the room. …

Shif T. ran back into the office, pushing open the door. Once again, it slammed into me. I was as flat as a slice of American cheese. I slid to the floor.

"Good news, Stilton," Shif T. said. "I found my cell phone. I left it in the bathroom."

 Chew on it!

Which of the following nouns are countable, and which are uncountable? opportunity, air, rodent, glasses

In each blank, write "C" if the noun is countable and "U" if it is uncountable.

1.	anger	_____	11.	office	_____
2.	beach	_____	12.	ornament	_____
3.	cheese	_____	13.	problem	_____
4.	city	_____	14.	proposal	_____
5.	corner	_____	15.	reporter	_____
6.	ear	_____	16.	salt	_____
7.	friend	_____	17.	silence	_____
8.	happiness	_____	18.	squeak	_____
9.	lightning	_____	19.	window	_____
10.	neck	_____	20.	wool	_____

© 2016 Scholastic Education International (S) Pte Ltd   ISBN 978-981-4629-95-9

Excerpt from *Watch Your Whiskers, Stilton!*
(Originally published in Italy by Edizioni Piemme *Attenti ai baffi … arriva Topigoni*)

When You Get Right Down to It...

 Fill in each blank with a suitable noun from the box below. For Mousella, use only countable nouns. For Kreamy, use only uncountable nouns.

jacket	understanding	energy	faith	cup	tail
help	success	sandwiches	calls	money	ears

I'm worried about Geronimo. He has not eaten his

_____. His _____
    1   2

of tea is untouched. He looks untidy. His tie is crooked. His

_____ is crumpled. He hasn't answered
        3

any _____ on his phone. He looks sad.
            4

His _____ is dragging behind him. Even
        5

his two _____ are drooping!
            6

Mousella MacMouser

Geronimo's not in the best of health at the moment. He has no

_____ to do anything; he is discouraged.
        7

The newspaper is in danger of closing down. We don't have

enough _____ to even pay the staff. We
            8

need to get some _____ from somewhere
                9

or someone. Nonetheless, I have _____
                                    10

in Geronimo. He has a good _____ of
                                11

what will work and what will not. I believe we can do well and

enjoy _____ again!
        12

Kreamy O'Cheddar

 Excerpt from *Watch Your Whiskers, Stilton!*
(Originally published in Italy by Edizioni Piemme *Attenti ai baffi ... arriva Topigoni*)

© 2016 Scholastic Education International (S) Pte Ltd ISBN 978-981-4629-95-9

Some nouns can be both countable and uncountable, e.g. glass, smell.

Countable:	**She asked for a <u>glass</u> of water.**
	There is a <u>smell</u> coming from the room.
Uncountable:	**That figure is made of <u>glass</u>.**
	He has a very good sense of <u>smell</u>.

For each of the underlined nouns below, write "C" for those that are countable and "U" for those that are uncountable.

Thea and Benjamin took Geronimo to a coffee <u>shop</u> to cheer him up.
₁

When they sat down, the <u>waitress</u> asked if they would like <u>coffee</u>, <u>tea</u>
₂   ₃   ₄

or <u>water</u>. Thea ordered two <u>cups</u> of tea and a <u>bottle</u> of water.
₅   ₆   ₇

When they got back to the <u>office</u>, Shif T. Paws was already working
₈

his <u>magic</u>. Geronimo's <u>mood</u> had lifted. He stood up and spoke to his
₉   ₁₀

<u>staff</u>. He gave them an inspiring <u>speech</u>. As he spoke, they all felt the
₁₁   ₁₂

<u>gloom</u> lifting. Benjamin felt that his uncle was a <u>joy</u> to listen to. When
₁₃   ₁₄

Geronimo finished speaking, everyone cheered with loud <u>claps</u>.
                                      ₁₅

1. _____
2. _____
3. _____
4. _____
5. _____
6. _____
7. _____
8. _____
9. _____
10. _____
11. _____
12. _____
13. _____
14. _____
15. _____

Hurrah for The Rodent's Gazette!

© 2016 Scholastic Education International (S) Pte Ltd ISBN 978-981-4629-95-9

Excerpt from *Watch Your Whiskers, Stilton!*
(Originally published in Italy by Edizioni Piemme Attenti ai baffi … arriva Topigoni)

3 The Mousetrap

To make a big pile of cash, Shif T. Paws signed me up as a contestant on *The Mousetrap*, a gameshow on which I could lose my tail!

The idea of going on a live game show, in front of millions of rodents, made my fur stand on end.

Bagel gave me another piece of *HOT* cheese bread to cheer me **up**. He tucked a third into my jacket pocket. "You never know," he said. "You may get hungry later."

But I didn't feel like eating. My tummy was doing flip-flops. Shif T. Paws dragged me out of the bakery and drove me to the television studio. I think he was AFRAID I would try to run away at the last minute. I hate to say it, but he was right! …

My tail trembled as the assistant led us into the studio. He took us to the host of the show, Vlad Torturetail. …

I *TURNED PALE*. I tried to sneak toward the exit, but Shif T. Paws pulled me **back**. …

Shif T. lowered his voice. "Come on, Stilton. What's more important? Your tail or *The Rodent's Gazette*?" …

I tried to slip away again, but this time Torturetail grabbed me. By the tail!

"You can't escape," he hissed. "The studio doors are locked. **THE TRAP IS READY!**" …

Suddenly, the lights in the studio went out. A big grandfather clock began striking the hours.

Subject-verb agreement means that subjects and verbs must agree in number. **Singular subjects** need singular verbs, e.g. **He was** afraid.; **It is** an honor to meet you.

Plural subjects need plural verbs, e.g. The **lights are** out.; **They were** victims.

Be sure to identify the subject correctly. Be careful of:

- words that end with "s" as they may not be plural nouns, e.g. spectacles; Geronimo's **pair of spectacles was** dirty.

- **compound subjects** that are formed with connectors like "and", "or", "nor", e.g. **Thea and Benjamin are** related.; **Either Thea or Benjamin is** going on the trip.

- inverted sentences where the verb

 Excerpt from *Watch Your Whiskers, Stilton!* (Originally published in Italy by Edizioni Piemme *Attenti ai baffi … arriva Topigoni*) © 2016 Scholastic Education International (S) Pte Ltd ISBN 978-981-4629-95-9

The Mousetrap

One . . . two . . . three . . . four . . . five . . . six . . . seven . . . eight . . . nine . . . ten . . . eleven . . . twelve . . . Twelve strokes. It was midnight!

The lights came. back on. I blinked. Two sturdy rats grabbed me.

"Your hour has come, Stilton!" they growled.

They dragged me toward a huge mousetrap. It looked like every rodent's worst nightmare. But I didn't try to fight them. It was too late to turn back now!

comes before the subject, e.g. There **is** a fly in my soup.; There **are** flies in my soup.

Chew on it!

Would you use a singular or plural verb with "millions of rodents" and "*The Rodent's Gazette*"? Why?

A. Complete each sentence with "is" or "are".

1. Thea and Benjamin _____ at the door.

2. A can of cheese crackers _____ on the table.

3. A bouquet of red roses _____ Thea's favorite.

4. The stress _____ too much for Geronimo.

B. Circle the correct verb.

1. The sacks of flour (is / are) heavy.

2. Bagel Buckwheat, the baker, (is / are) Mousella's cousin.

3. Geronimo (was / were) tired after trying to sell papers on the street.

4. Vlad Torturetail and Shif T. Paws (refuses / refuse) to let Geronimo leave the studio.

5. Everyone in the studio (waits / wait) for the contestant to lose his tail.

6. There (is / are) many members in the game show jury.

7. As Bagel hands out cheese bread, Shif T. (calculates / calculate) the day's takings.

8. "Thea or Benjamin (has / have) to persuade Geronimo," said Mousella.

© 2016 Scholastic Education International (S) Pte Ltd ISBN 978-981-4629-95-9   Excerpt from *Watch Your Whiskers, Stilton!* (Originally published in Italy by Edizioni Piemme *Attenti ai baffi … arriva Topigoni*) **15**

Underline the subject and circle the verb.

1. Here are the papers Thea wanted.

2. Shif T. Paws stands on a huge sack of flour.

3. In the long fancy car, Mrs. Smugrat takes out a coin.

4. The smell of freshly-baked bread fills the air.

5. Mousella always has some blue cheese nearby.

6. Neither mouse knows how to get out of there.

7. The group of VIP rodents comes into New Mouse City.

8. The stocky rat with the big muscular arms beats the gong.

9. Thea, Kreamy, and Mousella are waiting to speak with Geronimo.

10. The rats slip Geronimo's tail under the spring of the mousetrap.

  Excerpt from *Watch Your Whiskers, Stilton!*
(Originally published in Italy by Edizioni Piemme *Attenti ai baffi ... arriva Topigoni*)   © 2016 Scholastic Education International (S) Pte Ltd ISBN 978-981-4629-95-9

The 🐭 Mousetrap

A. Identify the subject in each sentence below. If the subject agrees with the verb, put a tick (✓) in the blank. If it does not, circle the wrong subject, and write the correct form of the subject in the blank. The sentences are all to be in the present tense.

1. The member of the game show jury do not look friendly. _____

2. The look on their faces make him feel uneasy. _____

3. Shif T. Paws wants Geronimo to win a million dollars. _____

4. Geronimo and Vlad stare at each other. _____

5. As he sees the director rubbing his hands in glee, they realizes the ratings are probably going up. _____

6. C. Offin looks like she might have a hive in her hair. _____

7. There is a very hostile look on S.H. Iver's face. _____

8. The piles of coins on the stand is just part of the prize. _____

B. Complete what Geronimo says using the words in brackets. Everything is to be in the present tense. Use the text on pages 14–15 to help you.

I really don't feel like eating. My _____
_____ (tummy, flip-flops). I _____
_____ (nervous). I do not want to go on the
game show. Shif T. Paws _____
_____ (afraid, will run away)

Excerpt from *Watch Your Whiskers, Stilton!*
(Originally published in Italy by Edizioni Piemme *Attenti ai baffi … arriva Topigoni*)

SELL! SELL! S-E-L-L!

To raise money, Shif T. Paws wants to explore new ways to sell. He gives six targets.

A.   Rewrite the sentences changing the plural nouns to singular ones.

FIRST TARGET:
We stand at the entrances of supermarkets and shopping malls. We sell to ladies while they shop for fruits and cheese.

_____

_____

_____

_____

SECOND TARGET:
We stand at traffic lights and sell to mice in their cars. Don't worry if the wives only buy two items from us.

_____

_____

_____

_____

B.   State if the underlined words are countable or uncountable nouns. The first one has been done for you.

THIRD TARGET:
We stand at train and subway <u>stations</u> and sell to <u>rodents</u> on the go. We can even sell in the <u>trains</u>. Our <u>spirits</u> will be lifted when the <u>money</u> comes in.

stations: countable
_____

_____

_____

FOURTH TARGET:
We walk in the <u>sunshine</u>, going to every <u>house</u>. We ask to borrow a cup of <u>sugar</u> or maybe some <u>coffee</u> before asking them to buy a <u>paper</u>.

_____

_____

_____

_____

Excerpt from *Watch Your Whiskers, Stilton!*
(Originally published in Italy by Edizioni Piemme *Attenti ai baffi ... arriva Topigoni*)

© 2016 Scholastic Education International (S) Pte Ltd ISBN 978-981-4629-95-9

C. **Underline the verbs that do not agree with their subjects. Then write the correct verbs above the wrong ones.**

FIFTH TARGET:

Rodents getting their fur tanned does not want to move from their cosy spots. However, they needs to read too! We goes to all the beaches. We looks for these rodents. We sells directly to them. This are service at its best! Everyone are happy!

SIXTH TARGET:

Mice loves to watch movies. There is plenty of them at the theater. We sells to them before the movie starts. We gets them to buy when the movie end. Comedies or romantic movies puts them in a good mood. The end of such movies are a good time to get them to buy.

© 2016 Scholastic Education International (S) Pte Ltd ISBN 978-981-4629-95-9

Excerpt from *Watch Your Whiskers, Stilton!*
(Originally published in Italy by Edizioni Piemme *Attenti ai baffi … arriva Topigoni*)

4 A Most Bizarre Mouse

My sister, Thea, forced me to go on a family trip to Pirate Islands.

A small hydroplane was waiting to take us to a place called Loot Island. According to my guidebook, the island was small and totally uncivilized. That meant no lights. No running water. No cheese logs by the pool. I sighed. Oh, how I love a nice cheddar cheese log.

My thoughts were interrupted by a most bizarre-looking rodent. ...

"The name's ROUGH RAT RICKY, but everyone calls me BOUNCER," he announced.

He squeezed my paw so hard, my eyes nearly popped out of my fur. Rancid rat hairs! That mouse had some shake. He was crushing every bone in my paw! I wouldn't be able to write for weeks!

I was about to complain when I noticed his tattoos. ...

Bouncer bounded onto the hydroplane. He patted a photo on the dashboard with his stubby paw. It was a picture of an older female mouse with hair just like Bouncer's. "Hi, **MOMSY WOMSY!**" he cooed. He blew the picture a kiss. Then he stared at the controls. "Frozen cheddar cheese pops!" he shrieked suddenly. "I've forgotten how to turn on the engine!"

I AM BOUNCER'S MOM.

The **infinitive** is the base form of a verb e.g. "be", "have", "sing", or "eat". When you add the word "to" in front, it is called the **to-infinitive**.

You use the to-infinitive:

- to express purpose, e.g. A plane was waiting **to take** us.

- after some verbs, usually those of thinking, feeling and saying, e.g. I <u>forgot</u> **to get** gas.

- after some question words (how, what, when, where, which), e.g. I've forgotten <u>how</u> **to turn on** the engine.

- after some nouns or pronouns to show what something can or will be used for, e.g. Geronimo needs a <u>pen</u> **to write** with.

 Excerpt from *Shipwreck on the Pirate Islands* (Originally published in Italy by Edizioni Piemme L'isola del tesoro fantasma)

 ISBN 978-981-4629-95-9

A Most Bizarre Mouse

My jaw hit the ground. "Wh-wh-what d-d-did you s-s-s-say?" I stammered.

Bouncer winked at me. "Just pulling your paw, Mousey Mouse!" he chuckled. ...

Suddenly, Bouncer stuck his head out of the window. He waved a paw at everybody on the runway. "SCRAM! MOVE IT! GET LOST!" he shrieked. Then he turned on the plane, and we shot off into the sky.

As soon as we were airborne, he smacked his forehead with his paw. "Cheese niblets!" he squeaked. "I forgot to get gas!"

My stomach dropped. "No g-g-gas?" I stammered.

Bouncer roared with laughter. "Just pulling your paw, Mousey Mouse!"

- after some adjectives to give a reason for the adjective, e.g. Geronimo was afraid **to get on** the plane.

Chew on it!

In the first sentence, is "to a place" considered a to-infinitive? Why?

 Fill in each blank with a to-infinitive of the verb in brackets.

1. Thea had _____ (force) Geronimo to go on a vacation to Pirate Islands.

2. Benjamin was excited _____ (go) on a trip with his uncle.

3. Geronimo barely had time to decide what _____ (take) with him.

4. When they landed thirteen hours later, Geronimo was happy _____ (get off) the plane.

5. Trap's presence made his cousin want _____ (leave) for home.

6. Bouncer called the control tower _____ (check) on the weather.

7. Geronimo was worried as the sky started _____ (grow) cloudy.

8. The last thing he wanted was _____ (fly) into a thunderstorm.

© 2016 Scholastic Education International (S) Pte Ltd ISBN 978-981-4629-95-9

Excerpt from *Shipwreck on the Pirate Islands*
(Originally published in Italy by Edizioni Piemme *L'isola del tesoro fantasma*) **21**

A. The to-infinitive can also be used with some adjectives to express an opinion. For example, "Geronimo found it impossible to believe anything that Trap said." Underline the correct answer in the sentences below.

1. Bouncer was odd (to be looking / to look) at.

2. It is easy (to love / to be loved) Benjamin because he is a kind mouse.

3. Thea needed something hard (to slap / to be slapping) Geronimo with.

5. Trap thought he was clever (to trick / to be tricked) his cousin.

6. Bouncer remembered clearly (to be checked / to check) the controls before taking off.

B. Rewrite the sentences below, correcting the error in each one. The first three errors have been identified for you.

1. Geronimo continued to read the guidebook <u>learning</u> about the different islands.

_____

Littlecocoa

2. Some islands like Littlecocoa, remain uninhabited and no one has gone to <u>settling</u> there.

_____

3. There are some islands that are dangerous <u>visited</u>, such as the shark-infested Fin's Revenge.

_____

Motormeltdown

4. Others like Motormeltdown, have strong currents that can cause ships crashing against the cliffs.

_____

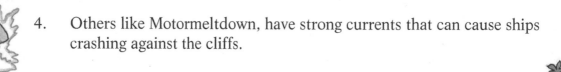

5. There are also islands that are very small and no one has tried went to, such as No Mouse's Land.

No Mouse's Land

_____

Thump Flop

6. Finally, there is Thump Flop, the home of the Plop birds, which no airplane dares flying to.

_____

 Excerpt from *Shipwreck on the Pirate Islands*
(Originally published in Italy by Edizioni Piemme L'isola del tesoro fantasma)   ISBN 978-981-4629-95-9

A.   **Fill in each blank with either a verb or a to-infinitive of the word in brackets.**

1.   Please _____ (fasten) your seat belts
     when you are in the plane.

2.   Bouncer decided _____ (blow) a kiss
     to his mother.

3.   Geronimo locked the door _____
     (keep) Trap out of his office.

4.   "Do not _____ (tease) your cousin," Trap was told.

5.   Benjamin was astonished _____ (see) his uncle being so brave.

6.   Geronimo was surprised _____ (read) about Pirate Islands

     and _____ (learn) that pirates have a code.

B.   **To make a negative to-infinitive, you include "not" before the "to". For example: "They tried not to laugh when Geronimo fell." Complete the sentences below with the to-infinitive. Write at least two in the negative.**

1.   Geronimo was prepared _____

     _____

2.   Trap bought some chocolate _____

     _____

3.   Bouncer was pleased _____

     _____

4.   Looking in the mirror, he was not sure which _____

     _____

5.   Thea would have preferred _____

     _____

6.   She was reminded _____

     _____

Excerpt from *Shipwreck on the Pirate Islands*
(Originally published in Italy by Edizioni Piemme *L'isola del tesoro fantasma*)

We were in the plane when the sky turned completely dark. Then we heard the Control Tower over radio, "Tor-na-do…".

I helped Benjamin put on a life jacket.

No one was talking. How unusual. Normally, you can't get the Stilton family to stop squeaking. Everyone stared worriedly at the sky. It grew **darker** and **darker**.

The wind blew furiously. The plane lurched and swayed.

SWISH…SWISHH…SWISHHH…

I held on to Benjamin's tiny paw for dear life.

"Don't worry, little nephew," I whispered. "We'll be just fine." I hoped he couldn't hear my teeth chattering. Or see my fur standing on end. Or feel my paw trembling. Rat-munching rattlesnakes! I was scared silly!

Suddenly, Bouncer pointed the plane's nose toward land.

"Hang on!" he screamed. "I'm going to try to make an EMERGENCY landing!"

The wind grew stronger and stronger. The waves grew closer and closer.

Adverbs modify verbs, adjectives, or other adverbs. Adverbs give us more information.

Adverbs of manner tell us *how* something happens. For example, if asked *how* the wind blew, we are told, "The wind blew *furiously*."

Adverbs of manner:

- usually end with "–ly", but there are some that do not, e.g. They worked **hard**.; He drives **fast**.

- are usually used with action verbs, e.g. stared, blew, pointed

- are usually placed after the main verb, e.g. Everyone stared **worriedly**.

Excerpt from *Shipwreck on the Pirate Islands*
(Originally published in Italy by Edizioni Piemme *L'isola del tesoro fantasma*)

© 2016 Scholastic Education International (S) Pte Ltd ISBN 978-981-4629-95-9

Nose Down into the Deep Blue Waves

Seconds later, a gust of wind sent the plane plunging *into the deep blue waves.*

The plane crashed into the sea with a loud splash. Instantly, we began to sink. GLUB . . . BLUB, BLUB, BLUB!

We tried to open the door. It wouldn't budge.

Then I remembered something I had read in one of my favorite books. In the book, the hero accidentally drives off a bridge. His car sinks underwater. The water pressure is too strong for him to escape. He has to wait until the car goes completely under.

Before long, the water had covered our plane. I pushed with all of my strength. And the door opened! Isn't reading amazing?

• cannot be placed between the verb and its direct object. So it is incorrect to say, "The hero drives off accidentally a bridge". It has to come before the verb OR after the object. "The hero accidentally drives off the bridge." or "The hero drives off the bridge accidentally".

Chew on it!

Do you think "underwater" is an adverb of manner in the sentence "His car sinks underwater."? Why?

Circle the adverbs of manner in the sentences below.

1. Benjamin waited patiently for his uncle to arrive.

2. He packed his luggage well, making sure he had everything he needed.

3. Geronimo ran fast to catch up with his sister.

4. He stared hard at the instructions Thea gave him, unsure where to go.

5. Bouncer looked menacingly scary.

6. The plane nosedived perilously into the sea.

7. They tried desperately to open the door.

8. They could only go out when the plane was completely filled with water.

9. Geronimo hurriedly grabbed Benjamin's paw, and hurled him roughly into the water.

10. Sighting land in the distance, they swam quickly to the island.

© 2016 Scholastic Education International (S) Pte Ltd   ISBN 978-981-4629-95-9

Excerpt from *Shipwreck on the Pirate Islands*
(Originally published in Italy by Edizioni Piemme *L'isola del tesoro fantasma*)

Fill in each blank with a suitable word from the boxes.

anxiously	slowly	thankfully

Geronimo took a long hard breath when he broke the surface of the water. He crawled

_____ onto the beach. Behind him was Benjamin. Their arms and legs felt
1

heavy like logs. _____, they looked out to sea for the other passengers.
2

Two heads soon popped out. _____, it was Thea and Trap. Bouncer,
3

however, was still missing.

continuously	diligently	exasperatingly	quietly	hard

Thea and Trap swam to land. They all gathered under a coconut tree. Everyone stood

there _____. No one uttered a word. Without warning, Trap
4

started to sob. Fat drops of tears rolled _____ down his face.
5

Thea rolled her eyes. She knew how _____ dramatic her
6

cousin could get. She rapped him _____ on the head, and
7

he gave a loud yelp. She then rallied everyone together. They came up with

a list of chores, and they were soon working _____ at their assigned tasks.
8

Geronimo built a shelter. Thea gathered wood for a fire. Benjamin made skirts out of

palm leaves as their clothes were soaking wet. Trap looked around for food.

invitingly	deservedly	quickly	suddenly

Once the shelter was done, Geronimo _____ took a break.
9

He looked out to sea. The waters looked _____ cool.
10

_____, seagulls started flying overhead. It caught him by surprise.
11

Benjamin _____ handed out little leaf-umbrellas to everyone.
12

He wanted to protect them from anything falling from the sky.

 Excerpt from *Shipwreck on the Pirate Islands*
(Originally published in Italy by Edizioni Piemme *L'isola del tesoro fantasma*)

© 2016 Scholastic Education International (S) Pte Ltd ISBN 978-981-4629-95-9

A. **In the sentences below, the adverbs of manner are in the wrong position. Circle the adverb, and draw an arrow from the circle to the place where the adverb should be.**

1. Before his trip, Geronimo had read eagerly up about Pirate Islands.

2. He guessed that correctly they were stranded on Thump Flop Island.

3. The guidebook said there was a aimlessly ghost wandering on the island.

4. The famous pirate Silverpaw had buried secretly treasure on the island.

5. Trap teased the recklessly crabs he found in the thick horribly mangrove forest.

6. Geronimo walked in the cautiously forest as he deathly was afraid of bumping into strange creatures.

B. **Form sentences with the given verbs (V) and adverbs of manner (Adv). You may use any form of the given verbs.**

1. V: find; Adv: bravely

   _____

   _____

2. V: step; Adv: carelessly

   _____

   _____

3. V: wave; Adv: painfully

   _____

   _____

   _____

4. V: walk, look; Adv: straight, slowly

   _____

   _____

   _____

© 2016 Scholastic Education International (S) Pte Ltd ISBN 978-981-4629-95-9 Excerpt from *Shipwreck on the Pirate Islands* (Originally published in Italy by Edizioni Piemme *L'isola del tesoro fantasma*) **27**

A peculiar sound had kept me awake for several nights. I'm sure it was a ghost! This time I had a plan on how to catch it …

I opened my eyes really wide. I had never seen a real live ghost before. Sure, I've had lots of near misses. Like when I was trapped in an old mansion that appeared to be haunted by cats. …

My fur stood on end. My knees felt weak. Then I noticed something strange. Bouncer wasn't floating in the air. And you couldn't see through his body. In fact, he looked just like he always did.

"Ho, ho, ho! I'm no ghost, Mousey Mouse!" Bouncer snickered. "You've been reading too many spooky stories!" …

That night, we celebrated Bouncer's return with a delicious meal. Here's the menu:

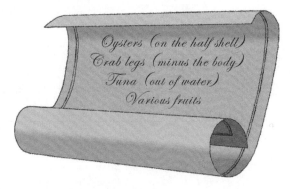

Oysters (on the half shell)
Crab legs (minus the body)
Tuna (out of water)
Various fruits

I licked my whiskers. Cheesecake! I was so hungry, my tummy was rumbling in three different languages. I decided to start with the oysters. But when I bit into one, I heard a horrifying CRUNCH! …

The **present perfect tense** is formed by using the present tense "has" or "have" with the past participle of a verb, e.g. has chased, have decided, have frozen.

You get the past participle of most verbs by adding "-d" or "-ed", e.g.
divide → divided
look → looked

Some verbs are different, e.g.
cut → cut
do → done
have → had

You use the present perfect tense:

• for something that began in the past and continues in the present, e.g. Geronimo **has been** a scaredy mouse all his life.; They **have run** this route many times, and they still enjoy it.

Excerpt from *Shipwreck on the Pirate Islands*
(Originally published in Italy by Edizioni Piemme L'isola del tesoro fantasma)

I shrieked. I had **CHIPPED** my tooth on something. I spit the nasty object into my paw. I could hardly believe my eyes. There in my paw lay an enormouse, glittering white pearl! …

The next morning, Trap woke me up at dawn. "Wake up, Geronimoid!" he shouted in my ear. "I've decided we need to go *SWIMMING*. No, make that YOU need to go *Swimming*." Uh-oh. I didn't like the sound of this.

"We need to find more oysters," Trap went on. "More oysters. More pearls. Got it, Germeister?"

I chewed my whiskers. "Why me?" I mumbled. "Why can't you go?"

Trap shook his head. "Well, isn't that just like you, Cousin? So self-centered. You need to learn to be a team player," he scolded. "Now, I've divided our jobs. You dive for the pearls. And I'll stay on the beach and watch."

• for an action that happened in the past, but is important at the time of speaking, e.g. I **have divided** the jobs.

 Chew on it!

"You've been reading too many spooky stories!" Is this an example of the present perfect tense? Why?

 Fill in the crossword with the past participle form of the clues.

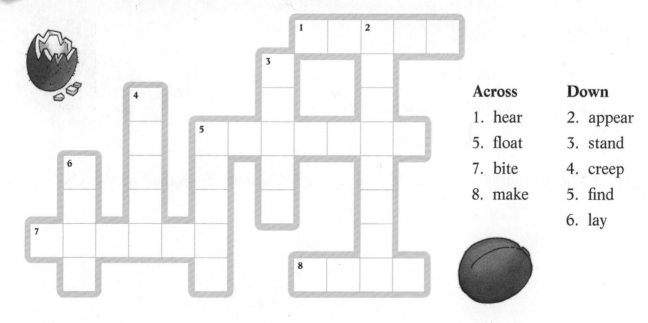

Across
1. hear
5. float
7. bite
8. make

Down
2. appear
3. stand
4. creep
5. find
6. lay

© 2016 Scholastic Education International (S) Pte Ltd ISBN 978-981-4629-95-9

Excerpt from *Shipwreck on the Pirate Islands*
(Originally published in Italy by Edizioni Piemme *L'isola del tesoro fantasma*)

A.   Circle the correct past participle in each sentence.

1.   Geronimo has (woke / woken) up after a nap.

2.   Something has (hit / hitting) Geronimo in the face.

3.   Trap has (threw / thrown) something at his cousin!

4.   The giant crab has (catch / caught) Geronimo in its pincer.

5.   Geronimo was chased by a giant crab and has (ran / run) in the other direction.

6.   In his panic, he has not (saw / seen) the root and has tripped on it.

7.   The Stiltons have (walk / walked) along the sandy path, and have (head / headed) into the mangrove forest.

8.   Huge holes have (open / opened) up, and crabs have (crawl / crawled) out of them.

B.   Fill in each blank with the present perfect tense of the word in brackets.

1.   Thea and Benjamin _____ (try) to distract the giant crab.

2.   It _____ (fling) Geronimo into the air and he _____ (land) in the partridge's nest.

3.   The mother partridge _____ (drop) a fat, juicy worm into Geronimo's mouth. He _____ (spit) it out.

4.   The baby birds _____ (eject) Geronimo from their nest and he _____ (fall) to the ground.

 Excerpt from *Shipwreck on the Pirate Islands*
(Originally published in Italy by Edizioni Piemme *L'isola del tesoro fantasma*)

© 2016 Scholastic Education International (S) Pte Ltd ISBN 978-981-4629-95-9

Oysters on the Half Shell

**Rewrite the sentences below in the present perfect tense.
Do not change the underlined words.**

1. Geronimo hears a weird "thump-flop" sound every night.

   _____

   _____

2. Bouncer lives on the other side of the island.

   _____

   _____

3. Trap decides that they <u>should hunt</u> for more oysters.

   _____

   _____

4. He sends Geronimo into the ocean.

   _____

   _____

5. Geronimo dives into the freezing water.

   _____

   _____

6. He finds a gazillion oysters and throws as many as he can into the basket.

   _____

   _____

7. Geronimo eats the oyster and bites into a pearl.

   _____

   _____

8. Geronimo surfaces, and Trap warns him about a shark!

   _____

   _____

© 2016 Scholastic Education International (S) Pte Ltd ISBN 978-981-4629-95-9
Excerpt from *Shipwreck on the Pirate Islands*
(Originally published in Italy by Edizioni Piemme *L'isola del tesoro fantasma*)

Help! Save Me!

Fill in each blank with either a to-infinitive, a verb in the present perfect tense, or an adverb of manner of the word in brackets.

1

Geronimo _____ (begin)

to swim like a maniac. He needs

_____ (get) away

from the shark! He hopes it cannot hear his heart beating

_____ (wild) in his chest.

2

Suddenly he hears Bouncer shouting

_____ (loud). "I am coming

_____ (help) you!" he yelled.

The next thing he sees is Bouncer jumping

_____ (purposeful) off the cliff.

Excerpt from *Shipwreck on the Pirate Islands*
(Originally published in Italy by Edizioni Piemme *L'isola del tesoro fantasma*)

© 2016 Scholastic Education International (S) Pte Ltd   ISBN 978-981-4629-95-9

3 Bouncer _____ (do) a cannonball dive off the cliff. He _____ (land) on the shark's back! A great crash can be heard ringing _____ (deafening) through the forest. The shark _____ (have) the wind knocked out of it.

4 As the shark begins _____ (snore), Geronimo reaches the beach. He is lucky to still be alive. He sighs _____ (grateful). Trap, however, says, "You _____ (take) your time to get back, haven't you?"

Excerpt from *Shipwreck on the Pirate Islands*
(Originally published in Italy by Edizioni Piemme L'isola del tesoro fantasma)

I needed an assistant to help me with my workload. Pinky Pick's résumé was impressive so I hired her. What I didn't realize was that she was only fourteen!

I shook my snout. "That is too young to work at a newspaper."

"That's what you think," she said. She held up one shocking-pink foot. "I wear size **twelve** shoes. I bet my paws are bigger than anyone's on your staff. Bigger than yours, even." ...

Cheese nips! This little mouse was starting to get on my nerves.

"Listen, young lady," I said. "I need a true professional to be my assistant. Not a little mouselet like you. Now, please run along." ...

Pinky smiled. She pulled a piece of paper out of her backpack and WAVED it in front of my snout. It was a contract made out to Pinky Pick. And there was my signature, *Geronimo Stilton*, right on the bottom!

"You see, Boss?" Pinky said. "You are so busy, you don't even know what you are signing. That is why you need a good assistant like me." ...

I sighed. Of course, I could not take this little mouse seriously. But I *did* have a problem. ...

Demonstrative determiners are used to modify nouns. They are usually placed before nouns. There are four of them:

- **this** and **these**: to indicate people or things near to the speaker
- **that** and **those**: to indicate people or things far away from the speaker

"This" and "that" are used for singular nouns while "these" and "those" are for plural nouns.

Demonstrative pronouns are the same four words, but used in a different manner. They are used to replace nouns or noun phrases, e.g. in:

- "**That** is too young to work at a newspaper", the word "that" is used to replace Pinky's age of fourteen

Excerpt from *My Name is Stilton, Geronimo Stilton*
(Originally published in Italy by Edizioni Piemme *Il mio nome è Stilton, Geronimo Stilton*)

© 2016 Scholastic Education International (S) Pte Ltd ISBN 978-981-4629-95-9

What's the 🗞 Problem, Boss?

I am not a big fan of Fuzzy Fuzzborn's. As I said before, I don't like loud rock music. But he is one of the most popular mice on Mouse Island. An interview with Fuzzy would be great for *The Rodent's Gazette*. There was only one problem.

"Fuzzy never gives interviews," I told Pinky. "He is a pretty cranky rat. Not even *you* could handle this one. No one can! I will find something else." …

"ONE INTERVIEW, COMING UP!" she cried.

I tried to jump out of the way. But there was no time.

That little mouse skated right over my tail!

• "**That**'s what you think", the word "that" is used to replace Geronimo's opinion that fourteen is too young for someone to work at the newspaper.

🧀 **Chew on it!**

"Not even you could handle this one." Do you think the word "this" is a demonstrative determiner or pronoun? Why?

🧀 **A. Fill in each blank with a suitable demonstrative determiner.**

1. Geronimo walked down the long hallway to his office. "_____ hallway needs some sprucing up," he thought.

2. "_____ flowers are lovely," said Benjamin, sniffing them as he spoke. "I'll get them for my Aunt Thea."

3. _____ little mouse over there made Geronimo's head spin.

4. Thea could not understand why _____ men in the far corner kept whispering when she walked past.

B. Circle the correct demonstrative pronoun.

1. Pinky's dressing is a little outrageous, but (this / these) does not mean that she can't do a good job.

2. Mousella had a smirk on her face and (that / those) made Geronimo suspicious.

3. Benjamin only had good thoughts about his uncle and (that / those) made Geronimo love him even more.

Excerpt from *My Name is Stilton, Geronimo Stilton*
© 2016 Scholastic Education International (S) Pte Ltd ISBN 978-981-4629-95-9   (Originally published in Italy by Edizioni Piemme *Il mio nome è Stilton, Geronimo Stilton*)

What's the Problem, Boss?

In the passage below, underline the demonstrative determiners and circle the demonstrative pronouns.

Geronimo needed an assistant. That was because he just had too many things to do. He read through all the résumés. When he got to Pinky's, he thought, "This person is just the right person for me!" With that, he hired her without an interview. Mousella, Geronimo's secretary, tried to warn him. "These whiskers of mine never lie," he said and refused to listen to her anymore.

Pinky arrived the next day and was shown to Geronimo's office. "Who's this?" he thought to himself. The young mouse wore enormouse shoes. These were shocking pink high-top sneakers with high, see-through platform soles. Those soles had pink plastic fish swimming in water! A bright light flashed on and off, illuminating those fish.

That wasn't all. The rest of her outfit was just as ridiculous. She wore a large yellow sweatshirt that was dotted with Swiss Cheese holes. Under this, she wore bright green leggings.

In addition to this, she had a clear plastic backpack on her back. From this dangled a diary covered in fake cat fur. This matched her shoes and was a shocking pink. Her backpack was clamped shut with a big lock shaped like a cat's head, but papers and photos stuck out from that.

 Excerpt from *My Name is Stilton, Geronimo Stilton*
(Originally published in Italy by Edizioni Piemme *Il mio nome è Stilton, Geronimo Stilton*)

© 2016 Scholastic Education International (S) Pte Ltd ISBN 978-981-4629-95-9

A. **Look at the picture below. Imagine you are Geronimo. Write three to four sentences using all four demonstrative determiners.**

_____

_____

_____

_____

_____

B. **Complete each sentence using the given demonstrative pronoun.**

1. Pinky may be young, but _____

_____ (this)

2. Mousella had tried to warn Geronimo many times, but _____

_____ (that)

3. Pinky found information on a very rare cheese, and also interviewed Fuzzy Fuzzborn.

_____

_____ (these)

4. Geronimo felt he hired the wrong person. Also, he saw a few things in the office he was not too pleased about.

_____

_____ (those)

Excerpt from *My Name is Stilton, Geronimo Stilton*
(Originally published in Italy by Edizioni Piemme *Il mio nome è Stilton, Geronimo Stilton*)

8 The Assistant's Assistant

By some miracle, Fuzzy Fuzzborn not only granted Pinky an interview, but also wanted her to write his biography. Now she had another surprise up her sleeve …

"I have NEWS, Boss!" she squeaked.

"NEWS about Fuzzy?" I asked hopefully.

"No, there is more NEWS," she said. "Come on, ask me what it is."

"All right, Pinky," I said. "What is it?" …

A small female mouse stepped out from behind Pinky. She looked like she was about fourteen, too.

"WHO ARE YOU?" I asked.

"My name is Merry Melody," she said shyly.

"Shouldn't you be in school?" I asked.

Pinky laughed. "It's CHRISTMAS vacation! There is no school. By the way, this is Merry—my new assistant!"

"Assistant!" I shouted. "Who said you were allowed to have an assistant?" …

"Hmm," she said, punching in numbers. "With Merry's help, I could write Fuzzy's biography faster. I could do it in one month instead of two!" …

I had no choice. I had to hire Merry or lose Pinky—and Fuzzy Fuzzborn—to *The Daily Rat*.

Interrogative pronouns are always used to ask questions.

As the word "pronoun" suggests, it takes the place of a noun, but this noun is unknown at the time the question is asked, e.g. **What** is it?

Interrogative pronouns consist of:

- Who, Whom, Whose (refer to people)
- What (refers to things)
- Which (refers to people or things).

Excerpt from *My Name is Stilton, Geronimo Stilton*
(Originally published in Italy by Edizioni Piemme *Il mio nome è Stilton, Geronimo Stilton*)

© 2016 Scholastic Education International (S) Pte Ltd ISBN 978-981-4629-95-9

The morning had been much too exciting for me. I wanted to forget about Pinky Pick—just for a little while. So later that day, I called a meeting of my staff at the publishing house.

I asked my sales manager for a report. "We need to make new products," Shif T. Paws said. "Something MODERN. Something exciting. Something for today's youth." ...

Pinky Pick ran into the room, carrying a stack of papers.

"How about a diary with cheese-scented pages? A series of biographies on rock singers? Or a backpack on wheels?" she asked. "And here's the best idea of all. We should publish a magazine for young mice. We can call it Fur Kids Only. And I think the right rodent for the job is . . . me!"

Chew on it!

Is the question word in "How about a diary with cheese-scented pages?" an interrogative pronoun? Why?

 A. **Circle the correct interrogative pronoun.**

1. (What / To whom) did they send the cheese?

2. (Whom / Whose) yellow sweater with Swiss cheese holes is this?

3. (Who / Which) did Geronimo hire?

4. (Whose / What) do you think about Geronimo's new assistant?

5. (Who / Which) story should they publish first?

B. **Match the correct interrogative pronoun with the rest of the question.**

1. What   •   • does the pink diary belong?

2. To whom •   • keys haven't been found?

3. Which   •   • did Thea say about her brother?

4. Whose   •   • gave Mousella permission to hire Pinky?

5. Who   •   • rock star did Pinky interview?

© 2016 Scholastic Education International (S) Pte Ltd ISBN 978-981-4629-95-9

Excerpt from *My Name is Stilton, Geronimo Stilton*
(Originally published in Italy by Edizioni Piemme *Il mio nome è Stilton, Geronimo Stilton*)

A. **Underline the interrogative pronouns below. Are they used correctly? If they are, put a tick (✓) in the blank. If not, write the correct interrogative pronoun in the blank.**

1. Whom photograph did Pinky have in her backpack? _____

2. Which course of action did Mousella decide to take? _____

3. Whose did Benjamin do with the special cheese tarts he received? _____

4. Whose is the name of the cheese that comes from Little Cheeseville? _____

5. Which said that Fuzzy Fuzzborn is a cranky mouse? _____

6. What was Thea speaking with just now? _____

7. Whose big feet can fit into those shoes? _____

8. Which does Geronimo suggest Pinky interview next? _____

B. **Fill in each blank with a suitable interrogative pronoun.**

1. _____ did Pinky say to Geronimo to calm him down?

2. _____ do you think Thea would prefer: the green or purple one?

3. _____ brought these wonderful mozarella chocolates to the office?

4. _____ bright idea was it to play a joke on Geronimo?

5. _____ did they see when they walked into the building?

6. _____ trouble has Geronimo gotten into now?

7. _____ is Geronimo related to?

8. _____ mouse in the group has volunteered to tell him the truth?

 Excerpt from *My Name is Stilton, Geronimo Stilton*
(Originally published in Italy by Edizioni Piemme *Il mio nome è Stilton, Geronimo Stilton*) © 2016 Scholastic Education International (S) Pte Ltd ISBN 978-981-4629-95-9

The Assistant's Assistant

 Use interrogative pronouns to form questions for the answers below.

1. Q: _____ did Geronimo decide yesterday?

   A: Yesterday, Geronimo decided he wanted to hire an assistant.

2. Q: _____ is his new assistant?

   A: Pinky Pick is his new assistant.

3. Q: _____ rodent is this present for?

   A: This present is for Geronimo's favorite nephew, Benjamin.

4. Q: _____

   A: The idea is Pinky's.

5. Q: _____

   A: Pinky interviewed Fuzzy Fuzzborn, the famous rock star.

6. Q: _____

   A: This scarf belongs to Mousella.

7. Q: _____

   A: Benjamin would prefer this book about castles to that one about trains.

8. Q: _____

   A: The weather forecast says that it will be bright and sunny.

© 2016 Scholastic Education International (S) Pte Ltd ISBN 978-981-4629-95-9

Excerpt from *My Name is Stilton, Geronimo Stilton*
(Originally published in Italy by Edizioni Piemme *Il mio nome è Stilton, Geronimo Stilton*)

9 Happy Birthday, Stilton!

It had been a disastrous day. Pinky decided to redecorate my office and made it very colorful. Then I got orange paint all over me. What would happen next?

It took me all day to wash the orange paint out of my fur. I went home that night in a **bad mood**.

Not only was my office ruined, but it was
Ⓜ︎Ⓨ︎ Ⓑ︎Ⓘ︎Ⓡ︎Ⓣ︎Ⓗ︎Ⓓ︎Ⓐ︎Ⓨ︎!
And nobody had remembered!

Now, I don't like to make a big deal of my birthday. A nice, quiet celebration is just fine. But I had not even received a single phone call. …

A few minutes later, I slumped up the stairs of my building. I unlocked my door and pushed it open.

Suddenly, the lights came on.

"HAPPY BIRTHDAY!" …

About a hundred mice filled my house! They all began to sing:

> May you have a happy day.
> Raise your snout and shout, "Hooray!"
> Now it's time to celebrate,
> Because your assistant is really great!

Your assistant is really great? What kind of birthday song was that?

Suddenly, I understood. …

Adjectives are describing words that tell us more about nouns.

Adjectives can commonly be found in front of nouns, e.g. **orange** paint; **nice**, **quiet** celebration.

Adjectives can also be placed after linking verbs such as forms of the verb "be", "become", "seem", "grow", e.g.

Geronimo is **upset**.; They are both **loud**.; That old gray mouse hole of yours was so **depressing**.

Excerpt from *My Name is Stilton, Geronimo Stilton*
(Originally published in Italy by Edizioni Piemme *Il mio nome è Stilton, Geronimo Stilton*)

© 2016 Scholastic Education International (S) Pte Ltd ISBN 978-981-4629-95-9

Happy Birthday, Stilton!

"Aha!" I cried. Pinky was behind this party. And I knew that could *not* be good!

Thea grabbed me. "Hey, Germeister," she said. "This party was a great idea! And it's all thanks to Pinky."

Thea gave *Pinky* a hug. Then it hit me.

Thea and Pinky are a lot alike! They are both loud. And they both like to stir up trouble. …

Suddenly, I felt a slap on my back. …

I turned around. It was my cousin Trap, of course.

"It's about time Y O U H A D A P A R T Y, Gerry Berry," he said. "That assistant of yours is good for you. I love your new office. That old gray mouse hole of yours was so depressing."

"But I *liked* my gray mouse hole!" I protested.

Chew on it!

Pick out all the other adjectives that are in front of nouns.

 Sometimes, the adjective(s) can come at the start of a sentence, e.g. "Tired, Geronimo made his way back home." Circle the adjectives in the sentences below.

1. Geronimo was upset that no one had remembered his birthday.

2. He climbed the dreary steps to his apartment.

3. The birthday boy was greeted by the smiling faces of his staff.

4. Suspicious, he looked around to see who was responsible for the celebration.

5. Geronimo groaned as his cheerful and annoying cousin, Trap, chattered on about him being such a grouchy person.

6. The loud music made him feel even more agitated.

7. Grateful for her help, Thea gave Pinky a big hug.

8. Benjamin would like to speak with Pinky, but he is a shy mouse.

Excerpt from *My Name is Stilton, Geronimo Stilton*
(Originally published in Italy by Edizioni Piemme *Il mio nome è Stilton, Geronimo Stilton*)

Rearrange the words to form a sentence, ensuring that the adjectives and punctuation are in the right places.

1. Geronimo timid   Trap   called   always

    _____

    _____

2. cheddar-yellow   Geronimo   office   painted   his

    _____

    _____

3. Geronimo   busy but happy   a few day ago,   mouse   was a

    _____

    _____

4. was there   cautious   he   round   who   peered
    to see   the corner

    _____

    _____

5. very   happy   soothing   the old lady   his
    words   made

    _____

    _____

    _____

6. ran up   rickety   building   old   Benjamin
    the   stairs   the   of

    _____

    _____

    _____

Excerpt from *My Name is Stilton, Geronimo Stilton*
(Originally published in Italy by Edizioni Piemme *Il mio nome è Stilton, Geronimo Stilton*)

© 2016 Scholastic Education International (S) Pte Ltd ISBN 978-981-4629-95-9

Form sentences with the following adjectives, placing them in the position indicated in brackets.

1. delightful (in front of a noun)

    _____

    _____

2. unpleasant (in front of a noun)

    _____

    _____

3. strong, robust (in front of two separate nouns)

    _____

    _____

4. popular (after a linking verb)

    _____

    _____

5. great (after a linking verb)

    _____

    _____

6. disappointed (at the start of the sentence)

    _____

    _____

Excerpt from *My Name is Stilton, Geronimo Stilton*
(Originally published in Italy by Edizioni Piemme *Il mio nome è Stilton, Geronimo Stilton*)

Geronimo Makeover

First, Pinky redecorated Geronimo's office. Then she tried to change his dressing. Then she made him try on 103 pairs of sunglasses! Read through the conversation between Pinky (P) and Geronimo (G) as he tries on the different pairs. Fill in the blanks with (a) a demonstrative determiner or pronoun, (b) a sentence containing the adjective in brackets, or (c) a question containing an interrogative pronoun. For (c), let the punctuation be your guide.

P: Trust me Boss! You will look great with a new pair of stylish sunglasses!

G: Ok… _____ ?
                                                  1

P: That one makes you look like a clown.

       _____ one might be better. Try this.
                        2

G: _____ (gaudy)
                              3

P: Try them anyway. … Maybe you're right.

       _____ (pretty pink)
                              4

G: I'm not trying _____! They are pink which is
                                5

       really not my color.

         P: All right.

                _____ ?
                                        6

         G: I don't prefer either of them. Let me try

                _____ round ones over there.
                            7

         P: No, no, no … Try _____ round ones here.
                                              8

         G: But the ones here have such small lenses I can't

                see anything.

Excerpt from *My Name is Stilton, Geronimo Stilton*
(Originally published in Italy by Edizioni Piemme *Il mio nome è Stilton, Geronimo Stilton*)
© 2016 Scholastic Education International (S) Pte Ltd   ISBN 978-981-4629-95-9

P: Are you sure?

_____?
                                 9

G: Mirror? What mirror?

P: _____
                               10

(golden). It's hanging on the wall in front of you.

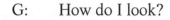

G: Well, I can't see it. Which tells me that _____
                                                        11

pair of sunglasses is not right for me.

P: I get it, Boss. Let's go to the next room. They have more choices there. …

_____
                        12

(trendy, green) Put them on.

G: How do I look?

P: Oh no! Maybe not. _____
                                        13

_____ (silly)

G: I'm beginning to think that there aren't any sunglasses that will

suit me.

P: Don't give up, Boss! _____
                                         14

_____ (not easy).

I'm sure we can get you a pair.

G: I appreciate your effort Pinky, but this is hopeless.

P: Wait! We haven't looked in the cupboard in that corner. _____
                                                                      15

_____ (wooden).

Excerpt from *My Name is Stilton, Geronimo Stilton*
(Originally published in Italy by Edizioni Piemme *Il mio nome è Stilton, Geronimo Stilton*)

I love running *The Rodent's Gazette*, but I needed a break. A vacation would be the perfect solution …

Blue skies… sandy beaches… I was dreaming of taking a vacation. Yes, I needed to escape the RAT RACE. I had been working so hard running the newspaper.

Oops, how rude. I almost forgot to introduce myself. My name is Stilton, *Geronimo Stilton*. I am the publisher of *The Rodent's Gazette*. It's the most popular paper on Mouse Island.

I love running the paper. But it is a lot of **work**. And all work and no play can make a mouse **very cranky**. At least that's what my great-uncle Happy Paws used to tell me. Anyway, one morning, I passed by some travel agencies on my way to the office. The pictures in the windows looked so relaxing. Palm trees, cheese bars by the pool…

I sighed. Yes, it was time to take a break.

I pushed open the door to **Kick Up Your Paws**. It's one of the best-known travel agencies in New Mouse City. But before I could step inside, someone pulled my tail.

"Why hello there, **Cousinkins!**" a voice screeched in my ear. "Going on vacation?"

Rats! It was my obnoxious cousin Trap. Now I definitely needed to get away. …

We use **quantifiers** to show how much or how many people or things there are.

Some quantifiers can be used with both countable and uncountable nouns. However, some can only be used with countable nouns, and others only with uncountable nouns:

- Countable: both, each, either, a few, few, fewer, neither, several

- Uncountable: a bit of, a little, little, much

- Both: all, any, enough, less, a lot of, lots of, more, most, no, none of, some.

Numbers such as "one" can also be used as quantifiers, e.g. I have **one** wish.

Excerpt from *Surf's Up, Geronimo!*
(Originally published in Italy by Edizioni Piemme *L'hai voluta la vacanza, Stilton?*)

© 2016 Scholastic Education International (S) Pte Ltd   ISBN 978-981-4629-95-9

Two seconds later, my cousin whipped out his cell phone. …

He paused to pick his nose, then continued. "No, he's nothing like me, Smoothie," he chuckled. "He's not into anything exciting. No SHARK fishing. No ROCK climbing. He's a total scaredy mouse. Yeah, a real TAIL TWIRLER. You know the type. He needs a little-old-lady vacation. Nothing more dangerous than some sunburned fur. Ha-ha. But he's got lots of money, so don't worry about the dough. The sky's the limit with this one!"

 Chew on it!

In Trap's statement "No, he's nothing like me, Smoothie,", do you think "no" is being used as a quantifier? Why?

 Circle a suitable quantifier for each sentence below.

1. The cats came face to face with (much / many) mice.

2. Thea bought (some / few) flour to make cheese bread.

3. (All / Much) persons were notified of the danger.

4. Geronimo likes (a few / a little) coffee to go with his biscuit.

5. (Most / A bit of) rodents are protected in this reserve.

6. The mice's faces showed (many / much) happiness.

7. (Little / Each) wall had paintings of famous rodents.

8. There was (several / enough) work to keep the rodents occupied.

9. The rodents could carry (fewer / less) rice than the cats.

10. Trap spilled (a few / much) coffee beans on the floor.

11. Benjamin found (a bit of / several) rulers in the box.

12. (A lot of / Fewer) litter was found in the subway.

Circle the incorrect quantifier in each sentence below. Then write suitable ones in the blanks.

1. Geronimo closed the blinds in his office as there was too many light.   _____

2. He walked around the office and spoke to a little of the staff.   _____

3. During lunchtime, he visited the café for any food.   _____

4. He wanted to read, and was happy that there was few noise around him.   _____

5. Feeling bored, Geronimo decided to have a walk for several exercise.   _____

6. He marveled at the much travel agencies that lined the street he was on.   _____

7. Two agencies had the vacation he was thinking of, and they were each located side by side.   _____

8. He stood between them, trying to decide on the neither options available.   _____

9. They either looked enticing, and Geronimo could not make up his mind.   _____

10. He only needed to pick any, but even that was difficult.   _____

Excerpt from Surf's Up, Geronimo!
(Originally published in Italy by Edizioni Piemme L'hai voluta la vacanza, Stilton?)
© 2016 Scholastic Education International (S) Pte Ltd ISBN 978-981-4629-95-9

Form sentences using suitable quantifiers for the nouns given. Do not repeat the quantifiers used.

1. sugar, tea

    _____

    _____

2. paper, pencils

    _____

    _____

3. cash, vacation

    _____

    _____

4. cheese, crackers

    _____

    _____

5. time, homework

    _____

    _____

6. children, milk

    _____

    _____

7. trees, beaches

    _____

    _____

8. people, apples

    _____

    _____

© 2016 Scholastic Education International (S) Pte Ltd ISBN 978-981-4629-95-9

Before I could protest, my cousin, Trap, dragged me to his friend's travel agency …

The mouse snickered when we came through the door. I wondered what was so funny. Then I stared at his outfit. Now *there* was something to laugh about. He was dressed in a loud Hawaiian-print shirt and shorts, even though it was THE MIDDLE OF WINTER! Dark sunglasses perched on his nose. A bracelet of green wooden beads dangled from his wrist. A tattoo on his right forepaw screamed **Aloha, Mousey**! …

I glanced around the room. It was packed with strange objects. They looked like souvenirs from around the world. An **ENORMOUSE** stuffed cat's head hung on one wall. I jumped. It looked so real! I saw a bow and a case filled with arrows. A small card next to the arrows warned:

CAREFUL, POISONOUS ARROWS!

I jumped again. Cheese niblets! This place was dangerous. Other CHEESY souvenirs filled the office. A large papier-mâché Buddha mouse sat on the mantelpiece. A collection of yellow rubber ducks from the *Quack Islands* lined one wall. A tacky

Adverbs of place tell us where something is taking place. They are usually placed after the main verb or the object of a sentence.

Adverbs of place can:

- be prepositions that tell us where someone or something is, e.g. perched **on** his nose, dangled **from** his wrist, **next to** the arrows, above, below, between, behind

- be directional, e.g. glanced **around**, slid back **inside**, up, down, north, towards, forward

- express the general idea of a location and end with the suffix "–where", e.g. somewhere; everywhere; nowhere.

Excerpt from *Surf's Up, Geronimo!*
(Originally published in Italy by Edizioni Piemme *L'hai voluta la vacanza, Stilton?*)

© 2016 Scholastic Education International (S) Pte Ltd ISBN 978-981-4629-95-9

sequined singing sombrero with blinking red lights lay on a desk. This place was like a flea market—a flea market filled with nothing but junk! …

Just then, an ear-piercing shriek filled the room. I **jumped** so high, I nearly hit the ceiling. Trap snickered. "See, Smoothie," he said to the sleazy-looking rodent, "I told you my cousin Geronimo is a scaredy mouse."

It was then that I noticed the plastic cuckoo clock. A sickly-looking bird had popped out of the clock door. It shrieked out the hour, then slid back inside.

Smoothie Slickpaws took off his sunglasses and shot me a sly smile. "WELL, HELLO, GERATTIMO!" he SHRIEKED, even louder than the cuckoo. …

Chew on it!

Find two prepositions that are not adverbs of place. How can you tell they are just prepositions?

Circle the adverbs of place in the sentences below.

1. Geronimo wanted to go somewhere for his vacation; anywhere peaceful and relaxing would be wonderful.

2. Unfortunately, before he could say anything, Trap took him to an alleyway nearby.

3. Geronimo stood outside the shabbiest-looking travel agency and peered through the window.

4. He saw a sleazy-looking rodent sitting behind a huge desk.

5. He was reluctant to enter, but Trap pushed him towards the door.

6. Geronimo had to walk between two huge statues to get in.

7. The whole place was cluttered. Even the ceiling above had things hanging from it.

8. As Trap spoke, Smoothie disappeared downstairs.

Hello, Gerattimo?

Fill in each blank with an adverb of place from the boxes. Each adverb should only be used once.

everywhere	there	ahead	outdoors

The longer Geronimo stayed in Smoothie's agency, the more upset he got. No matter

what he did, he kept seeing useless mementos _____. After a while,
                                                        1

he just kept looking straight _____ and did not dare to move his
                                        2

eyes very much. He was itching to get _____ as everything in
                                                3

the agency was so loud and gaudy. But Trap would not let him leave, so he was stuck

_____.
        4

under	in	by	above	towards

He saw a spider descend on its thread from the ceiling _____, drop
                                                                    5

to the ground, and scuttle _____ him. As it got nearer to him, it
                                    6

stopped _____ his shoe and looked at Geronimo before scurrying
                7

_____ the table. Geronimo stayed put _____
        8   9

his chair. He did not like spiders.

southwest	nowhere	upstairs

Smoothie had been down in the cellar for a long time. When he came back

_____, he began typing on his computer. He wanted to send
        10

Geronimo to the _____ (not the popular northeast) of
                        11

New Mouse City. He wanted him to visit San Shabby Fur

Island. Geronimo was, of course, not happy! The

island was in the middle of _____!
                                    12

Geronimo did not like where all this planning was going.

Excerpt from *Surf's Up, Geronimo!*
(Originally published in Italy by Edizioni Piemme *L'hai voluta la vacanza, Stilton?*)

© 2016 Scholastic Education International (S) Pte Ltd ISBN 978-981-4629-95-9

A.   Fill in the blanks with the correct adverb of place.

in front of	somewhere	next to	under

1.   Trap wanted Smoothie to send his cousin

_____ he had never been before.

2.   He stood _____ the cuckoo clock high up

on the wall and grinned.

3.   He watched Geronimo as his cousin stood

_____ Smoothie's desk, looking frustrated.

4.   Trap moved _____ Geronimo and waved

the brochure in his face.

B.   Form sentences with the adverbs of place given.

1.   behind

_____

_____

2.   below

_____

_____

3.   up

_____

_____

4.   nowhere

_____

_____

Smoothie booked me on a trip to San Shabby Fur Island, and I was to leave in two hours! I only had time to call Thea and Benjamin, then make my way to the airport …

At last, I climbed on board the plane. I was a little concerned. I had never flown LGA (Last Gasp Airways) before. …

I was wedged between an elderly lady and a young mouselet. …

The young mouse on my other side made faces at me. Then he stole the cream cheese candy the flight attendant had just offered me. …

Seconds later, Bratfur began PESTERING me with questions.

Meanwhile, Bratfur's mother shot me a proud smile. "MY LITTLE DARLING IS ALWAYS SO CURIOUS. …

I forced a smile. *Maybe I could take a nap*, I decided. But before I could even close my eyes, BRATFUR began chattering again. …

By now, my head was about to explode. I couldn't take it anymore. I pictured myself tossing Bratfur out the emergency exit. …

The flight attendant began to serve lunch.

Connectors are used to join groups of words or sentences together.

Connectors of time and sequence show the relationship between actions or situations:

- To introduce the first of two actions, we use "when", "as soon as", "the moment", or "before", e.g. "… **before** I could even close my eyes, …"

- To introduce the second of two actions, we use "after", "afterwards", "later", or "then", e.g. Seconds **later**, Bratfur…

- To introduce a series of actions or events in order, we use "first", "second", "third", "finally", etc, e.g. **First** Bratfur. **Now** the food.

- To show simultaneous actions, we use "while", "meanwhile",

 Excerpt from *Surf's Up, Geronimo!*
(Originally published in Italy by Edizioni Piemme *L'hai voluta la vacanza, Stilton?*)

I nibbled on a cracker. It tasted like cardboard.

Next I tried some **blue cheese soup**. It was **SOUR**.

I cut into the rubbery chicken. It slipped under my knife and landed in my suit pocket.

Sauce dribbled down my jacket. Oh, what a horrible flight! First Bratfur. Now the food.

"when", "while" or "as", e.g. **Meanwhile**, Bratfur's mother …

Chew on it!

"By now, my head was about to explode." Which of the four categories listed do you think "by now" falls into?

 Circle the correct connector of time and sequence.

1. (After / Before) Geronimo could protest, Smoothie had already booked his entire vacation.

2. (As soon as / Next) he got to the airport, Geronimo was ushered onto the plane.

3. Geronimo was about to relax when (suddenly / meanwhile), Bratfur launched into a series of questions.

4. (Since / After) they served lunch, they showed an in-flight movie.

5. Bratfur kept pestering Geronimo (firstly / while) he tried to sleep.

6. (Finally / Later), when the plane hit some turbulence, Geronimo reassured the elderly lady next to him.

7. (Subsequently / Previously), the plane continued to rock, and he began to feel sick and needed to throw up.

8. Geronimo began to panic (then / when) he saw Bratfur playing with his airsickness bag.

9. Unable to stop himself from throwing up, Geronimo (finally / after) had to yell for someone to give him a bag. But it was too late.

10. (By the time / While) they reached their destination, everyone wanted to get away from Geronimo.

💵 **Sometimes, some connectors of time and sequence overlap with connectors of addition, e.g. "in addition", "moreover", "furthermore". These connectors of addition can also be used to show sequence. Fill in each blank with a suitable connector given in brackets.**

1. This is the order in which Geronimo ate: _____, he nibbled on a cracker. _____, he tried the blue cheese soup. _____, he cut into the chicken. (afterward, first, then)

2. _____, Geronimo did not have enough time to pack for his trip. _____, he was not given a choice in his vacation destination. (moreover, this time)

3. _____ Bratfur was making so much noise, Geronimo thought he could shut him out by listening to music. _____ he put his headphones on, the little boy started talking even louder. Geronimo tried to be patient with Bratfur _____ he could not take it anymore. (until, the moment, since)

4. _____ to all the noise he had to endure, Geronimo had a horrible lunch. He felt ill. _____, he had to put up with turbulence. _____ the elderly woman beside him kept talking about food, he found it difficult not to throw up. _____, he could not control himself. He vomitted. (eventually, futhermore, in addition, when)

Excerpt from *Surf's Up, Geronimo!*
(Originally published in Italy by Edizioni Piemme *L'hai voluta la vacanza, Stilton?*)

Join the sentences given using suitable connectors of time and sequence from the box. Each connector should only be used once. Rewrite the sentences if necessary.

when	as soon as	the moment	first
next	while	since	then

1. The plane landed. Geronimo ran to the airport toilet.

    _____

    _____

2. Geronimo went to get his baggage. He went to see the customs mouse.
    He went to look for the mouse from the travel agency.

    _____

    _____

3. Geronimo could not find the agency mouse in the airport. He left the airport.

    _____

    _____

4. Geronimo saw a slimy-looking rat carrying a sign. He waved the rat over.

    _____

    _____

5. The slimy-looking rat saw Geronimo. The slimy-looking rat asked if he
    was "Gerattimo".

    _____

    _____

6. The slimy-looking rat looked Geronimo over.
    Geronimo took a deep breath and tried to remain calm.

    _____

    _____

© 2016 Scholastic Education International (S) Pte Ltd ISBN 978-981-4629-95-9   (Originally published in Italy by Edizioni Piemme *L'hai voluta la vacanza, Stilton?*)

POOR GERONIMO!

The plane had landed, but Geronimo's spate of bad luck continued even after he left the aircraft. Fill in each blank with either a quantifier (Q), an adverb of place (A), or a connector of time and sequence (C). Use the clues in brackets to help you.

1

The aircraft was on the ground. _____ (C) Geronimo
got down from the plane, his first thought was to get his suitcase.
He walked _____ (A) the baggage claim section.
On the way, a mouse with huge muscles ran over his tail with
a trolley carrying _____ (Q) suitcases.

OH, NO!

2

Geronimo grimaced in pain _____ (C) he
continued on his way. A lady mouse in high heels stomped on his
paw as she walked _____ (A) him. Geronimo was
in _____ (Q) pain before, but it was still bearable.
Now he was in _____ (Q) pain; he almost fainted!

OUCH!

3

_____ (C) he had orange juice
in his face! Bratfur had thrown a glass of juice
at him and now his best jacket was stained.

He-he-heee...

4

Geronimo went to the restroom to clean up. He took off his jacket and
hung it _____ (A) a hook so that he could wash his face.
He splashed only _____ (Q) water on his snout so that
his shirt would not get wet. _____ (C) he was in the
restroom, he dropped his passport into the toilet bowl!

HOLEY CHEESE!

from Surf's Up, Geronimo!
published in Italy by Edizioni Piemme L'hai voluta la vacanza, Stilton?)

5

It took a while for him to fish his passport out from the toilet bowl.

_____ (C) he finally reached the baggage claim section,
12

he was miserable. He sat down _____ (A) the baggage
13

carousel and started to cry. _____ (C) he realised
14

what was happening, the carousel started to move and his tail got

stuck in the gears! He was caught totally unawares!

HELPP!!!

6

_____ (C) Geronimo yanked his tail out
15

from the carousel, he looked for his suitcase. There were still

_____ (Q) bags on the carousel and he found
16

seven that looked like his. He and a female mouse both reached

for a bag at the same time. Geronimo recognized his tag. He

_____ (C) had to wrestle her for his bag.
17

IT'S MY SUITCASE!

7

_____ (C), Geronimo was ready to leave the airport.
18

He handed his passport to the customs mouse who looked

at it in disgust. His passport was stinky! Poor Geronimo!

He had so _____ (Q) bad things happen to him at
19

the start of his vacation. He walked slowly _____ (A)
20

the airport exit. He was already tired even before the vacation

began. Would things get better soon?

WHAT A STINK!

© 2011 Scholastic Education International (S) Pte Ltd ISBN 978-981-4629-95-9   (Originally published in Italy by Edizioni Piemme S.p.A.)

Answers

Unit 1
Pages 6–7
Chew on it! question:
trouble — troubles; speech — speeches; company — companies

Page 7
1. baby — babies
2. throat — throats
3. watch — watches
4. monkey — monkeys
5. tooth — teeth
6. cheese — cheeses
7. child — children
8. day — days
9. bus — buses
10. solution — solutions
11. race — races
12. city — cities

Page 8
A.
1. books
2. knives
3. newspapers
4. benches
5. daisies
6. shelves
7. squeaks
8. jokes

B.
1. deer
2. furniture
3. pants
4. species
5. salmon

Page 9
1. letters
2. voice
3. trees
4. leaves
5. carpet
6. bread
7. desk
8. scissors

Unit 2
Pages 10–11
Chew on it! question:
rodent, glasses, opportunity: countable; air: uncountable

Page 11
1. anger: U
2. beach: C
3. cheese: U
4. city: C
5. corner: C
6. ear: C
7. friend: C
8. happiness: U
9. lightning: U
10. neck: C
11. office: C
12. ornament: C
13. problem: C
14. proposal: C
15. reporter: C
16. salt: U
17. silence: U
18. squeak: C
19. window: C
20. wool: U

Page 12
1. sandwiches
2. cup
3. jacket
4. calls
5. tail
6. ears
7. energy
8. money
9. help
10. faith
11. understanding
12. success

Page 13
1. shop: C
2. waitress: C
3. coffee: U
4. tea: U
5. water: U
6. cups: C
7. bottle: C
8. office: C
9. magic: U
10. mood: U
11. staff: C
12. speech: C
13. gloom: U
14. joy: U
15. claps: C

Unit 3
Pages 14–15
Chew on it! question:
For "millions of rodents": plural (refers to many rodents); for *The Rodent's Gazette*: singular (refers to one publication)

Page 15
A.
1. are
2. is
3. is
4. is

B.
1. are
2. is
3. was
4. refuse
5. waits
6. are
7. calculates
8. has

Page 16
1. Here are the papers Thea (wanted).
2. Shif T. Paws (stands) on a huge sack of flour.
3. In the long fancy car, Mrs. Smugrat (takes out) a coin.
4. The smell of freshly baked bread (fills) the air.
5. Mousella always (has) some blue cheese nearby.
6. Neither mouse (knows) how to get out of there.
7. The group of VIP rodents (comes) into New Mouse City.
8. The stocky rat with the big muscular arms (beats) the gong.
9. Thea, Kreamy, and Mousella (wait) to speak with Geronimo.
10. The rats (slip) Geronimo's tail under the spring of the mousetrap.

Page 17
A.
1. members
2. looks
3. ✓
4. ✓
5. he (replacing "they")
6. ✓
7. ✓
8. are (replacing "is")

B. I really don't feel like eating. <u>My tummy is doing flip-flops.</u> <u>I feel/am feeling nervous.</u> I do not want to go on the game show. <u>Shif T. Paws is afraid that I will run away.</u>

Activity 1
Pages 18–19
A. First target:
I stand at the entrance of a supermarket and shopping mall. I sell to a lady while she shops for fruit and cheese.

Second Target:
I stand at the traffic light and sell to a mouse in his car. Don't worry if the wife only buys one item from me.

B. Third target:
rodents: countable; trains: countable; spirits: uncountable; money: uncountable

Fourth target:
sunshine: uncountable; house: countable; sugar: uncountable; coffee: uncountable; paper: countable (countable in this case as "paper" refers to "newspaper")

C. Fifth target:
Rodents getting their fur tanned <u>do</u> not want to move from their cosy spots. However, they <u>need</u> to read too! We <u>go</u> to all the beaches. We <u>look</u> for these rodents. We <u>sell</u> directly to them. This <u>is</u> service at its best! Everyone <u>is</u> happy!

Sixth target:
Mice <u>love</u> to watch movies. There <u>are</u> plenty of them at the theater. We <u>sell</u> to them before the movie starts. We <u>get</u> them to buy when the movie <u>ends</u>. Comedies or romantic movies <u>put</u> them in a good mood. The end of such movies <u>is</u> a good time to get them to buy.

Unit 4
Pages 20–21
Chew on it! question:
"To a place" is not a to-infinitive. The "to" here is not paired with a verb.

Page 21
1. to force
2. to go
3. to take
4. to get off
5. to leave
6. to check
7. to grow
8. to fly

Page 22
A.
1. to look
2. to love
3. to slap
4. to trick
5. to check

B.
1. Geronimo continued to read the guidebook <u>to learn</u> about the different islands.
2. Some islands like Littlecocoa, remain uninhabited and no one has gone <u>to settle</u> there.
3. There are some islands that are dangerous <u>to visit</u>, such as the shark-infested Fin's Revenge.
4. Others like Mortormeltdown, have strong currents that can cause ships <u>to crash</u> against the cliffs.
5. There are also islands that are very small and no one has tried <u>to go</u> to, such as No Mouse's Land.
6. Finally, there is Thump Flop, the home of the Plop birds, which no airplane dares <u>to fly</u> to.

Page 23
A.
1. fasten
2. to blow
3. to keep
4. tease
5. to see
6. to read; learn/to learn

B. Accept all reasonable answers.

Unit 5
Pages 24–25
Chew on it! question:
"Underwater" in this sentence is not an adverb of manner. It does not tell us <u>how</u> the car sank; it tell us <u>where</u> the car sank to.

Page 25
1. patiently
2. well
3. fast
4. hard
5. menacingly
6. perilously
7. desperately
8. completely
9. hurriedly; roughly
10. quickly

Page 26
1. slowly
2. Anxiously
3. Thankfully
4. quietly
5. continuously
6. exasperatingly
7. hard
8. diligently
9. deservedly
10. invitingly
11. Suddenly
12. quickly

Page 27
A. 1. eagerly read
2. guessed correctly
3. aimlessly wandering/wandering aimlessly
4. secretly buried
5. recklessly teased; horribly thick
6. walked cautiously; deathly afraid
B. Accept all reasonable answers.

Unit 6
Pages 28–29
Chew on it! question:
No because "have been reading" is in the present continuous tense. In the present perfect tense, the sentence would have been "You've read too many spooky stories!".

Pages 29
Across:
1. heard   5. floated   7. bitten   8. made
Down:
2. appeared   3. stood   4. crept   5. found   6. laid

Page 30
A. 1. woken
2. hit
3. thrown
4. caught
5. run
6. seen
7. walked; headed
8. opened; crawled
B. 1. have tried
2. has flung; has landed
3. has dropped; has spat
4. have ejected; has fallen

Page 31
1. Geronimo has heard a weird "thumb-flop" sound every night.
2. Bouncer has lived on the other side of the island.
3. Trap has decided that they should hunt for more oysters.
4. He has sent Geronimo into the ocean.
5. Geronimo has dived into the freezing water.
6. He has found a gazillion oysters and has thrown as many as he can into the basket.
7. Geronimo has eaten the oyster and has bitten into a pearl.
8. Geronimo has surfaced, and Trap has warned him about a shark!

Activity 2
Page 32–33
1. has begun; to get; wildly
2. loudly; to help; purposefully
3. has done; has landed; deafeningly; has had
4. to snore; gratefully; have taken

Unit 7
Pages 34–35
Chew on it! question:
In this sentence, "this" is a demonstrative determiner. It is used to modify the noun "one" (just like "this thing/person").

Pages 35
A. 1. This   2. These   3. That   4. those
B. 1. this   2. that   3. that

Page 36
Geronimo needed an assistant. That was because he just had too many things to do. He read through all the résumés. When he got to Pinky's, he thought, "This person is just the right person for me!" With that, he hired her without an interview. Mousella, Geronimo's secretary, tried to warn him. "These whiskers of mine never lie," he said and refused to listen to her anymore.

Pinky arrived the next day and was shown to Geronimo's office. "Who's this?" he thought to himself. The young mouse wore enormouse shoes. These were shocking pink high-top sneakers with high, see-through platform soles. Those soles had pink plastic fish swimming in water! A bright light flashed on and off, illuminating those fish.

That wasn't all. The rest of her outfit was just as ridiculous. She wore a large yellow sweatshirt that was dotted with Swiss Cheese holes. Under this, she wore bright green leggings.

In addition to this, she had a clear plastic backpack on her back. From this dangled a diary covered in fake cat fur. This matched her shoes, and was a shocking pink. Her backpack was clamped shut with a big lock shaped like a cat's head, but papers and photos stuck out from that.

Page 37
A. Accept all reasonable answers.
B. Accept all reasonable answers.

Unit 8
Pages 38–39
Chew on it! question:
No, it is not an interrogative pronoun. It does not refer to a noun.

Page 39
A. 1. To whom   2. Whose   3. Who
4. What   5. Which
B. 1. What did Thea say about her brother?
2. To whom does the pink diary belong?
3. Which rock start did Pinky interview?
4. Whose keys haven't been found?
5. Who gave Mouselle permission to hire Pinky?

Page 40
A. 1. Whom → Whose   2. Which (✓)
3. Whose → What   4. Whose → What
5. Which → Who   6. What → Who
7. Whose (✓)   8. Which → Who
B. 1. What   2. Which   3. Who   4. Whose
5. What/Who   6. What   7. Who   8. Which

Page 41
1. What   2. Who   3. Which
4. Whose idea is this?
5. Who did Pinky interview?
6. Who does this scarf belong to?/To whom does this scarf belong?/Who owns this scarf?
7. Which book would Benjamin prefer, this book about castles or the one about trains?
8. What does the weather forecast say?

Unit 9
Pages 42–43
Chew on it! question:
bad; big; single; happy; birthday; new

Page 43
1. upset
2. dreary
3. birthday; smiling
4. Suspicious
5. cheerful; annoying; grouchy
6. loud; agitated
7. Grateful; big
8. shy

Page 44
1. Trap always called Geronimo timid.
2. Geronimo painted his office cheddar-yellow.
3. A few days ago, Geronimo was a busy but happy mouse.
4. Cautious, he peered round the corner to see who was there.
5. His soothing words made the old lady very happy.
6. Benjamin ran up the rickety stairs of the old building. /
Benjamin ran up the rickety old stairs of the building. /
Benjamin ran up the old rickety stairs of the building.

Page 45
Accept all reasonable answers.

Activity 3
Pages 46–47
Accept all reasonable answers. Suggested answers:
P: Trust me Boss! You will look great with a new pair of stylish sunglasses!
G: Ok... Which pair should I try?
P: That one makes you look like a clown. This one might be better. Try this.

G: This pair seems very gaudy.
P: Try them anyway. … Maybe you're right. Try these pretty pink frames.
G: I'm not trying that! They are pink which is really not my color.
P: All right. What about these two pairs?
G: I don't prefer either of them. Let me try those round ones over there.
P: No, no, no… Try these round ones here.
G: But the ones here have such small lenses I can't see anything.
P: Are you sure? What about the mirror over there?
G: Mirror? What mirror?
P: The one with the golden frame. (golden) It's hanging on the wall in front of you.
G: Well, I can't see it. Which tells me that this pair of sunglasses is not right for me.
P: I get it, Boss. Let's go to the next room. They have more choices there. … Look at these trendy, green ones. Put them on.
G: How do I look?
P: Oh no! Maybe not. You look silly in these sunglasses.
G: I'm beginning to think that there aren't any sunglasses that will suit me.
P: Don't give up, Boss! Finding a pair that suits you and that you like is not easy. I'm sure we can get you a pair.
G: I appreciate your effort Pinky, but this is hopeless.
P: Wait! We haven't looked in the cupboard in that corner. That's the wooden cupboard over there.

Unit 10
Page 48–49
Chew on it! question:
No, it is not being used as a quantifier. It is not referring to any amount (of anything).

Page 49
1. many	2. some	3. All	4. a little
5. Most	6. much	7. Each	8. enough
9. less	10. a few	11. several	12. A lot of

Page 50
1. many → much
2. a little → a few/ some
3. any → some/a little
4. few → little
5. several → some/a little
6. much → many
7. each → both
8. neither → two
9. either → both
10. any → one

Page 51
Accept all reasonable answers.

Unit 11
Page 52–53
Chew on it! question:
These prepositions do not indicate place — "about" (paragraph 1): it is a preposition showing "on the subject of"; "with" (paragraph 2, 3): it is a preposition showing possession

Page 53
1. somewhere; anywhere	2. nearby
3. outside; through	4. behind
5. towards	6. between
7. above	8. downstairs

Page 54
1. everywhere	2. ahead	3. outdoors	4. there
5. above	6. towards	7. by	8. under
9. in	10. upstairs	11. southwest	12. nowhere

Page 55
A.
1. somewhere	2. under
3. next to	4. in front of

B. Accept all reasonable answers.

Unit 12
Page 56–57
Chew on it! question:
It falls into the second category—to introduce the second of two actions.

Page 57
1. Before	2. As soon as	3. suddenly
4. After	5. while	6. Later
7. Subsequently	8. when	9. finally
10. By the time		

Page 58
1. first; Then; Afterward
2. This time; Moreover
3. Since; The moment; until
4. In addition; Furthermore; When; Eventually

Page 59
Accept all reasonable answers. Suggested answers:
1. As soon as the plane landed, Geronimo ran to the airport toilet.
2. First, Geronimo went to get his baggage. Then he went to see the customs mouse. Next, he went to look for the mouse from the travel agency.
3. Since Geronimo could not find the agency mouse in the airport, he left.
4. The moment Geronimo saw a slimy-looking rat carrying a sign, he waved him over.
5. When the slimy-looking rat saw Geronimo, he asked if he was "Gerattimo".
6. Geronimo took a deep breath and tried to remain calm while the slimy-looking rat looked Geronimo over.

Activity 4
Pages 60–61
Accept all reasonable answers. Suggested answers:
1. The moment	2. to	3. a few	4. while
5. by	6. some	7. a lot of	8. Suddenly
9. on	10. a little	11. While	12. When
13. next to	14. Before	15. As soon as	16. many
17. then	18. Finally	19. many	20. towards